This book belongs to

_____

APPLE PIE and POEMS

Copyright © 2017 by Aletheia James

ISBN 13: 978-0-9979317-3-0
ISBN 10: 0-9979317-3-6
Library of Congress PCN 2017931233

All Rights Reserved. No parts of this book may be reproduced or utilized in any form or by any means, electronic or mechanical, including photocopying, scanning, recording, or by any information storage and retrieval system now known or hereafter invented, without permission, in writing from the publisher.

To contact Aletheia James or to order a copy of this book, please visit
www.amitypublications.com

Printed in the United States of America

Apple Pie and Poems

WRITTEN AND ILLUSTRATED BY

Aletheia James

One morning in mid-October, Lily headed outside to play under her favorite tree. She stood under the big birch, her black hair blowing in the wind. What a beautiful day. Lily loved to create poems. She thought...

Leaves
spiky, shiny
rustling, swinging, shining
nature, sun, tree, bark
swaying, gleaming, reaching
tall, smooth
birch.

Did you know...this poem is called a *diamante*?

It has seven lines and is written in the shape of a diamond. The 1st and 7th line have one noun. The 2nd and 6th line include two adjectives describing nouns closest to them. The 3rd and 5th line have three "ing" words related to those nouns. Line four has four nouns, two related to first one, two related to the last one.

It wasn't long before Lily heard her mom calling.
"Lily, I need you to peel some potatoes."
Lily ran back inside. She enjoyed helping her mom.
As she was peeling the potatoes,
another poem came to mind. She thought...

Sometimes when I'm sitting still,

As quiet as can be

I want to shout and bounce and run

As far as I can see.

Did you know...this poem is called a *simple rhyme*?

It has four lines at least two of which rhyme.
This one is made in the A B C B method.
B and B rhyme, but A and C do not.

After Lily finished peeling the potatoes, she walked
over to the window. Looking outside,
she saw the wind was blowing very hard.
As she watched the wind spinning, she thought...

On a very windy day,
The leaves all want to run and play.

Did you know...this poem is called a *couplet*?

It is made up of two lines that rhyme.

Once the wind stopped blowing, Lily told her mom she was heading outside again. She ran into the meadow and flopped onto the grass. As she looked up at the sky, she couldn't help but think of another poem. She thought...

Smiling, smiling

The sun comes smiling

Smiling as the day goes by.

Did you know...this poem is called **free verse**?

Free verse does not need to rhyme, does not need to have any format, but does have a free style rhythm.

After basking in the warm sun, Lily noticed a tall tree at the edge of the meadow. She decided to climb to the top. Looking around, she could see all the trees in autumn colors. She thought...

I see many trees

As far as the eye can see

Birch, Oak, Pine, and Beech.

Did you know...this poem is called a *haiku*?

It has five syllables for the first and third lines,
and seven syllables for the second line.

Suddenly Lily heard her mom call to her. "Lunch time, Lily!" Lily climbed down the tree, ran back to the house, washed her hands, and sat down to a delicious meal with oven browned potatoes. After lunch, Lily's mom started to gather the ingredients to make an apple pie, Lily's favorite dessert. That made her think of yet another poem. She thought...

There was an old man from Rye.

One day, he ate too much pie.

He said, "One more lick!

I'm sure to be sick!"

Said the old man from Rye.

Did you know...this poem is called a *limerick*?

The first, second, and fifth line rhyme with each other and have seven to ten syllables. The third and fourth line rhyme as well, but they can have only five to seven syllables.

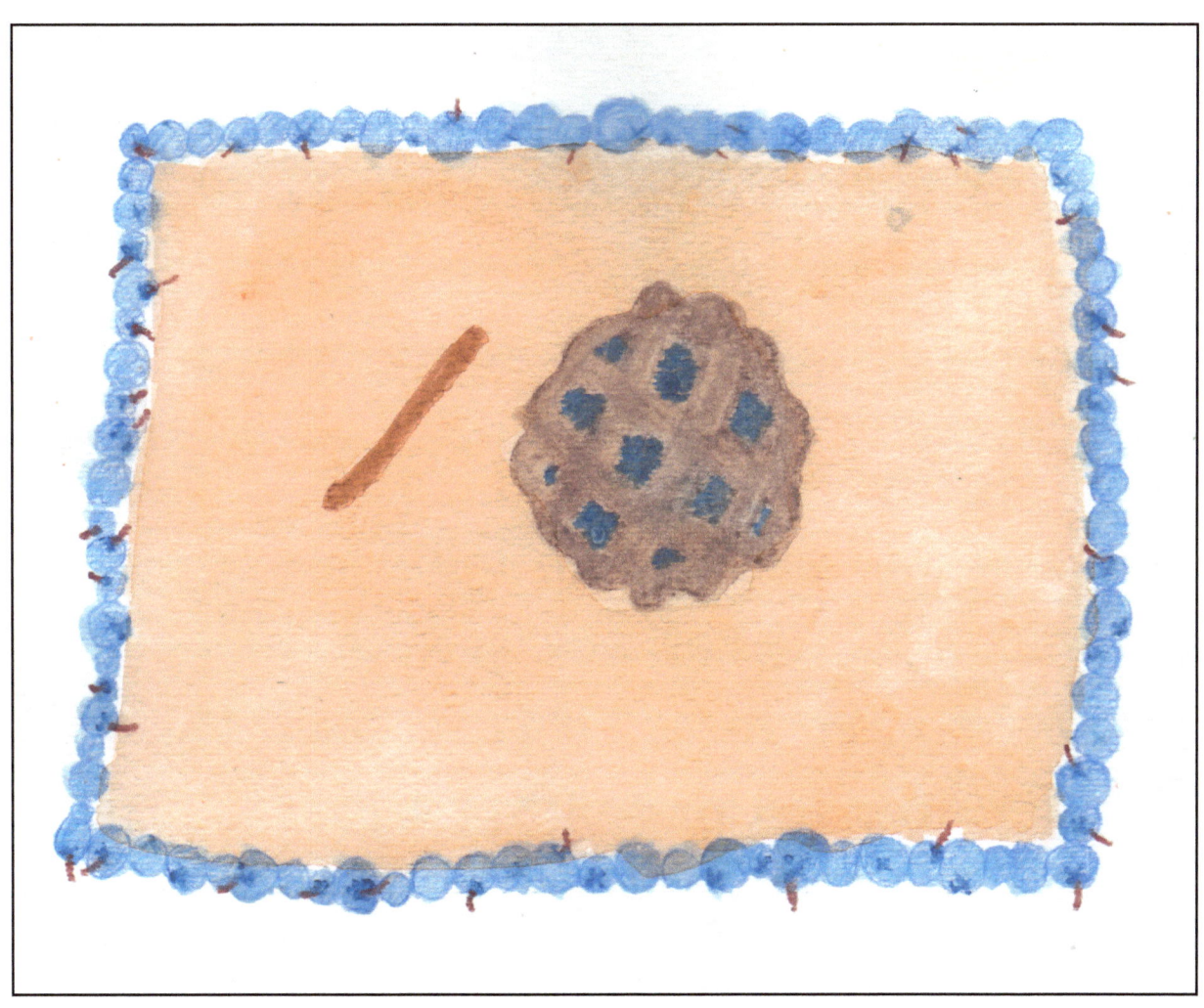

After lunch, Lily headed back outside to explore the woods. She came upon a tree sapling. It stood very straight and tall as if it was trying to reach the sun. As she looked up, another poem popped into her head. She thought...

Oh, there's many mighty pieces of rain
I'm at the bottom of a tree, the base
For I am now a very tiny grain
Yes, I'm a seed, of me there's not a trace.

I wish that I could go and run and run!
Or reach to the great blue and mighty sky
If I could I would go and touch the sun
Like the tall tree I reach my branches high.

And with the sun and rain I will now grow
I'll reach my branches way up from the ground
Now here I see there comes a great big hoe
It pushes the tall weeds into a mound.

Now look at how much I have grown, yes me
Look, I am just a very little tree.

Did you know...this poem is called a *sonnet*?

It consists of fourteen lines. They are made up of three stanzas, each having four lines and one stanza that has two lines. The four line stanzas are written in the ABAB rhyming pattern. The two line stanza is a couplet. There are five stressed and five unstressed syllables in each line. The first syllable of each line in not stressed. When you listen to it, you hear a stressed syllable every other syllable.

Lily noticed three little squirrels running up the trees. As she looked up, there were four cardinals hopping from branch to branch, chirping loudly. She thought...

Cardinals in their

Apt flash of

Red

Dance through the

Ink black

Night

And

Look,

See them take

Flight into the

Light of the moon

I see them

Greatly enjoy

Hopping and

Twittering

Did you know...this poem is called an *acrostic*?

The first letter of each line makes its own word or phrase vertically. An acrostic is very easy to write because it doesn't need to rhyme or have rhythm. Also, you can make each line as short or long as you want.

After watching the cardinals' antics for a while,
Lily walked to a nearby brook. She could see
the leaves falling into the stream. As she watched
the last leaf fall from a branch, she thought...

The wind blows through the town
I hang onto the trees
I am orange, yellow, and red
I'm falling, save me, please!

I'm falling on the wind
Floating to the ground
Unto the water I fall
There's water all around.

I floated down the stream
Bobbing up and down
I'm not a fish, I cannot swim
I do not want to drown.

But then a girl saw me here
She saw my colors bold
She picked me up and then she said,
"I have something to hold."

Now you've heard my story
So now guess what I am
I have no fins or noses
And I am not a lamb.

Did you know...this poem is called a *ballad*?

A ballad has at least four stanzas with four lines each.
A ballad is usually a story and has action.

The sun was setting and Lily knew that meant it was almost time for dinner. As she entered the kitchen, she could smell the apple pie baking in the oven. As soon as dinner was over, mom carried the dessert to the table. As they ate their apple pie, Lily recited her favorite type of poem.

We like to eat pie.

Mother makes it so yummy.

Soon the pie is gone.

Do you know what type of poem this is?

A Note from the Author

I attended a writer's workshop at my local library. One of the assignments was to draft a children's book about something I thought was important for children to know. Since I've always loved poetry and also enjoy illustrating, it seemed natural to combine the two. Add to that my love of baking apple pies with my mom and grandma, it all seemed to come together.

The picture on the cover is a pie I made with my mom. I thought you'd enjoy the recipe so I've added it to the end of this book. After all, the title says this book is about apple pie, too!

Theia James

Love That Apple Pie

Preheat oven to 450°

Crust

2 cups all-purpose flour
½ tsp. salt
2/3 cup shortening
6 to 7 tbsp. cold water

1. Stir flour and ½ tsp. salt
2. Cut in shortening with pastry blender until pieces are pea size.
3. Sprinkle 1 Tbsp. water, gently toss with a fork. Push moistened dough to side of bowl. Repeat, adding 1 Tbsp. of water at a time. Divide in half. Form each half into a ball.
4. On lightly floured surface, flatten a dough ball. Roll into a 12" circle.
5. Transfer pastry to pie plate.
6. Flatten and roll other ball into a 12" circle. Cut Into ½" wide strips.
7. After filling the crust with apple filling, place strips on top of filling.
8. Flute edges of pie crust by placing thumb against inside of pastry. Press dough around thumb with thumb and index finger from the other hand.

FILLING

Need About 6 apples, pared, cored and sliced; set aside

Combine:
½ cup sugar
1 tsp. Cinnamon
2 tbsp. flour
A pinch salt

1. Place crust in pie pan
2. Sprinkle half of the filling into crust
3. Add half of the apples
4. Sprinkle the remainder of the fill
5. Fill with remaining apples
6. Place the strips of crust on top

CRUMB TOPPING

¼ cup butter
½ cup sugar
1 tsp. cinnamon
¾ cup flour

1. Mix ingredients together
2. Spoon mixture onto pie
3. Bake for 10 minutes
4. Reduce temp. to 350°
5. Bake for 30 minutes

HOPE YOU ENJOYED
THIS BOOK AND MY APPLE PIE!

www.ingramcontent.com/pod-product-compliance
Lightning Source LLC
Chambersburg PA
CBHW041542040426
42446CB00002B/197